The Herb
& Spice Book
for Kids

Gifts to Make
Crazy Cure-Alls
Food Recipes
Growing Herbs

The Herb & Spice Book for Kids

Alice Siegel & Margo McLoone

illustrated by
Gwen Brodkin

Holt, Rinehart and Winston / New York

To George and Kathryn,
whose help made this possible,
and to our dear families
and friends.

Text copyright © 1978 by Alice Siegel and Margo McLoone. Illustrations copyright © 1978 by Gwen Brodkin.
All rights reserved, including the right to reproduce this book or portions thereof in any form. Published simultaneously in Canada by Holt, Rinehart and Winston of Canada, Limited. Printed in the United States of America.

10 9 8 7 6 5 4 3 2 1

Library of Congress Cataloging in Publication Data

Siegel, Alice.
    The herb & spice book for kids.

    SUMMARY: Discusses the cultivation and uses of a variety of common herbs.
    1. Herbs—Juvenile literature.   2. Nature craft—Juvenile literature.   3. Herbs
—Therapeutic use—Juvenile literature.   4. Herb gardening—Juvenile literature.
[1. Herbs. 2. Gardening. 3. Cookery—Herbs. 4. Handicraft] I. McLoone,
Margo, joint author.   II.   Brodkin, Gwen.   III.   Title.
TX406.S53   635′.7   77-26712   ISBN 0-03-041681-7

Contents

Introduction

This is a book to introduce you to the wonderful world of herbs and spices. If you like to do fun things and make easy treats, you will like this book.

Herbs are plants. We use them as perfumes, medicines and food flavorings. Spices are the seeds, roots, leaves and bark of certain herbs and trees. They are generally used only to season foods. But you will find many other uses for them in this book.

Today, as herbs and spices become more and more popular, you should have no trouble finding the ones called for here. The herbs and spices you'll need are probably already in your kitchen. If you have to buy any, they will be of additional use for everyday household purposes. Many herbs and spices are in your local supermarket, in the spice section. They appear in a variety of forms—as whole dried leaves or seeds, powdered or crushed—sometimes in liquid form. Some of the less-commonly-used herbs and spices can be found in health food stores, or may be ordered from a list of companies given at the end of this book. The best herbs are the fresh ones.

If you are a do-it-yourselfer, you can grow your own herbs. Herbs are the easiest and most pleasurable plants to grow. All you need is a sunny windowsill. You can grow herbs winter and summer, and your house will smell good all the time. If you are lucky enough to have a garden, you can also grow herbs outdoors. There are two types of herbs, perennial and annual, and the last chapter provides instructions on how to grow both kinds, along with simple directions on drying and storing.

Once you have your herbs and spices, put them to good use. If you tie a ribbon around almost any project in this book, you will find it will make a great gift. Some of the best gifts you can give are the ones you make yourself, and all the items we've chosen are easy and fun to make. In the food recipes section, you will see that ordinary foods become special with herbs and spices. You will also have fun making crazy cure-alls. Long before there were doctors and drugstores, people were using plants to ease aches and pains. The crazy cure-alls are not recommended for serious ailments, but they are certain to amuse you and your friends.

Here are only some of the hundreds of ways herbs and spices can be used. After you've tried these recipes, make up some gift ideas of your own!

Herbs and Spices

Basil 	Bayleaf 	Camomile 
Cinnamon 	Cloves 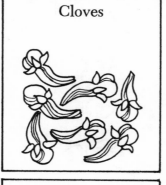	Comfrey 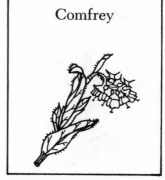
Coriander 	Dandelions 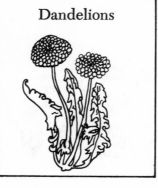	Dill 

Elder leaves	Feverfew	Garlic

Ginger	Juniper berries	Laurel leaves

Lavender	Lemon balm	Lovage
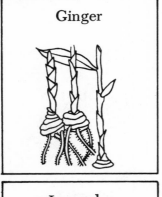		
Marjoram	Mint leaves	Nettle leaves
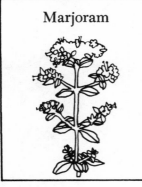		

Onion	Oregano	Parsley

Peppercorn	Rosemary	Saffron

Sage	Spearmint leaves	Strawberry leaves

Tansy	Tarragon	Thyme
		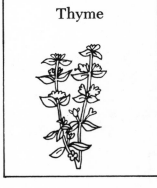

·I·
Gifts to Make

Herb Shampoo

What You Need

Ingredients
1 tablespoon olive oil
1 bottle castile soap
2 or 3 teaspoons of whichever
  herbs you choose:
  rosemary
  thyme
  lemon verbena
  ginger

Tools
large jar with lid
fine strainer
large spoon

What You Do

1. Pour oil, soap, and herbs in large jar.
2. Mix ingredients with spoon and put on lid.
3. Store in cool dark place for one week.
4. Pour through strainer. Use on hair or as a body shampoo.

Clove & Peppercorn Necklace

What You Need

Ingredients
1 cup cloves
1 cup peppercorns or allspice
juniper berries or rosehips
    for color

Tools
nylon transparent thread
scissors
needle

What You Do

1. Arrange cloves, peppercorns and other herbs on a table in the order you want them in the necklace.
2. Cut a piece of thread long enough so it will fit over your head after it is knotted.
3. Put thread through the needle and knot one end of the thread.
4. Pierce the cloves and peppercorns with needle and string them.
5. Tie the two ends together tightly.

Astrological Herb and Plant Chart

What You Need

Ingredients

Drawing of herbs, or pressed dried plants

Aries	Rosemary
Taurus	Lovage
Gemini	Tansy
Cancer	Lemon balm
Leo	Saffron
Virgo	Wheat
Libra	Strawberry leaves
Scorpio	Basil
Sagittarius	Feverfew
Capricorn	Comfrey
Aquarius	Parsley
Pisces	Seaweed

large piece of cardboard-like paper

clear contact paper or laminating paper

Tools

scissors

felt-tip pen

What You Do

1. Place the dried plants or the cut-out pictures of them on the chart.
2. Cover each picture with a piece of clear contact paper.
3. Label each picture with its name and sign.
4. Print the words ASTROLOGICAL HERB AND PLANT CHART across the top.

Astrological Herb and Plant Chart

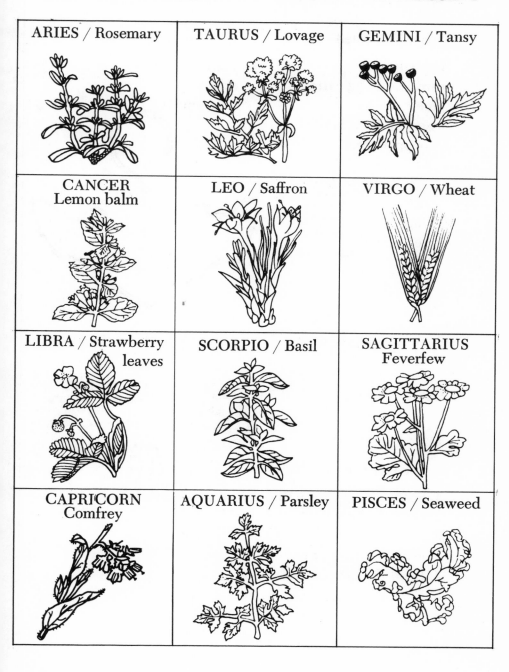

ARIES / Rosemary	TAURUS / Lovage	GEMINI / Tansy
CANCER Lemon balm	LEO / Saffron	VIRGO / Wheat
LIBRA / Strawberry leaves	SCORPIO / Basil	SAGITTARIUS Feverfew
CAPRICORN Comfrey	AQUARIUS / Parsley	PISCES / Seaweed

Mobile

What You Need

Ingredients
cardboard egg cartons
glue
assorted dried herbs
    peppercorns
    tarragon
    cinnamon bark
    coriander
string
wire hanger

Tools
scissors
hole punch

What You Do

1. Separate eggcups with scissors.
2. Glue the herbs onto the outside of the cups.
3. Punch holes in cups and pull string through, leaving a knot at the end.
4. Bend the hanger to a shape you like.
5. Tie the strings to the hanger.

Herb-Scented Candles

What You Need

Ingredients

1 square paraffin wax
2 teaspoons of your choice
  of herb oils or cinnamon,
  cloves, vanilla, peppermint
2 or 3 ordinary candles

Tools

deep cooking pot
large candleholder
tongs

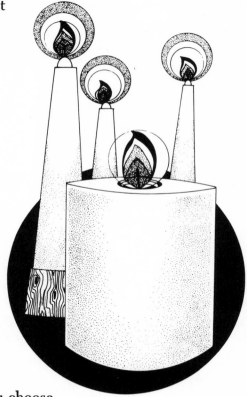

What You Do

1. Melt the wax in the pot.
2. Stir in whichever scent you choose.
3. Hold candles with tongs and dip into melted wax.
4. Place upright in candleholder until dry
   (candles will drip slightly).

Fresh Herb Planter

What You Need

Ingredients
porous rock (sandstone) or
   large seashell
potting soil—a little bit
small fresh potted herbs:
   parsley
   mint
   dill
   basil

Tools
penknife
spoon

What You Do

If using rock:
1. Use the knife to scrape a shape out of the rock.
2. Dig a hole in the rock.
3. With spoon, fill the hole with a little soil.
4. Plant herb in earth and water it.
5. Keep the rock on a saucer when watering.

If using shell:
1. Fill the shell with a little dirt.
2. Plant herb in earth and water it.
3. Keep the shell on a saucer when watering.

23

Pomander Balls

What You Need

Ingredients
1 thin-skinned orange
1 box cloves
2 teaspoons cinnamon
tissue paper
ribbon

Tools
scissors

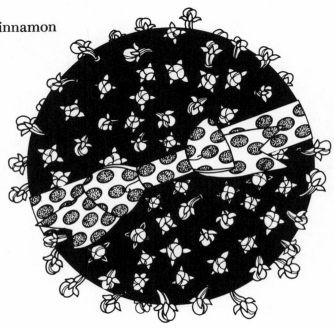

What You Do

1. Poke the cloves (pointed end) into the orange until the orange is completely covered.
2. Roll the orange in cinnamon.
3. Wrap in tissue paper and place in a cool dry place for several weeks.
4. Remove from paper and tie the ribbon around the orange.
5. Either hang in closet for scent or show for decoration.

Potpourri

What You Need

Ingredients
juniper berries
cloves
dried orange peel
dried lemon peel
cinnamon sticks
dried mint
bayleaf
jars with lids
ribbon

Tools
large mixing bowl
large spoon
scissors

What You Do

1. Mix all the herbs in mixing bowl.
2. Pour mixture into jars.
3. Tie ribbon around lid of each jar.

Home-Dyed T-Shirts

What You Need

Ingredients
20 whole dandelions
water
1 T-shirt (cotton)
hanger

Tools
cooking pots (2)
long spoon
strainer

What You Do

1. Take dandelions and put into pot of water.
   (Add more dandelions for deeper color.)
2. Boil for two hours, stirring occasionally.
3. Pour through strainer into second pot.
4. Put clean, dry, unfolded T-shirt into second pot
   and simmer for 30 minutes, stirring constantly.
5. Rinse in cool water until water runs clear.
6. Fold over hanger to dry.

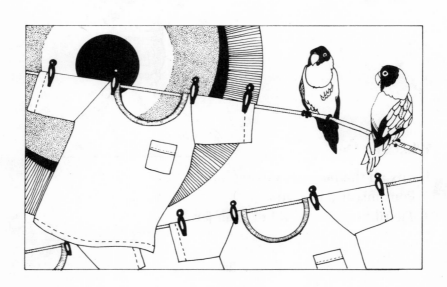

Home-Made Cards

What You Need

Ingredients   **Tools**
heavy paper   scissors
clear contact paper   pen
   (laminating paper)
dried herbs of your choice

What You Do

1. Cut paper to twice the card size wanted.
2. Cut piece of laminating paper to card size wanted.
3. Place the herb in the center of the *right* half of card.
4. Place contact paper over right half of card and rub to seal in herb.
5. Fold card in half and write your own message inside.

Meaning of Herbs:

Basil—"I don't like you."
Camomile—"I admire you."
Dill—"You cast a spell on me."
Fennel—"I'm sorry."
Lavender—"I want you as a friend."
Marjoram—"You make me happy."
Rosemary—"I won't forget you."
Thyme—"I admire your courage."

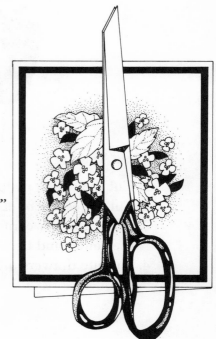

Sachets

What You Need

Ingredients
small pieces of cotton
   (muslin), 8″ x 8″
potpourri or any other
   combination of dried herbs
ribbon

Tools
scissors
ruler

What You Do

1. Cut the cotton material into small squares.
2. Fill the center of each square with potpourri.
3. Bring the four corners of the squares toward
   the center and tie with ribbon.
4. Put into drawers to keep clothes sweet-smelling.

Kitchen Herb Bouquet

What You Need

Ingredients
dried dill stalks
dried parsley sprigs
dried sage sprigs
dried basil sprigs
onion bulbs
garlic bulbs
pretty ribbons or cord,
   each about 7" long
piece of string 15" long

Tools
scissors

What You Do

1. Tie ribbons around the stems of each bunch
   of herbs and around the stalks of the bulbs.
2. String the herbs and bulbs together.
3. Hang them upside down as kitchen decoration.

Herb Terrarium

What You Need

Ingredients
sand
fish bowl
small pebbles
potting soil
fresh plants:
    parsley
    basil
    sage
small saucer or coffee-can lid

Tools
flour scoop or ladle
small spoon

What You Do

1. Pour sand into bottom of bowl.
2. Put a layer of pebbles over sand.
3. Fill in the bowl with rich potting soil.
4. Using the opposite end of spoon, make holes for the plants.
5. Insert your plants and water them well.
6. Put saucer or lid over bowl.
7. Mist whenever soil looks dry—about once a month.

Herbal Lip Balm

What You Need

Ingredients
2 tablespoons petroleum
   jelly (Vaseline)
1/8 teaspoon peppermint
   extract
1/8 teaspoon vanilla extract

Tools
small cooking pot
wooden spoon
table knife
small round plastic
   container with lid, or
   empty margarine tub

What You Do

1. Carefully melt the petroleum jelly in the pot over a low flame.
2. Add the peppermint and vanilla and stir with the wooden spoon. Cool a few minutes.
3. Pour the mixture into the plastic container and refrigerate for 5 to 10 minutes or until hardened.
4. Remove from the refrigerator. Use the knife to scoop out some of the balm and put it into a small container to carry with you. You may use a little pill box, an empty rouge container, or a small matchbox lined with aluminum foil.

This will soothe chapped lips.

Herb-Scented Stationery

What You Need

Ingredients

small piece of pretty fabric, about 4" x 8"

⅓ cup dried lavender or potpourri

Tools

scissors

needle

thread

What You Do

1. Cut the fabric into two squares of the same size. Make them about 4" x 4".
2. Sew the two pieces together on three sides.
3. Fill with lavender or potpourri.
4. Sew the bag closed.
5. Place in the bottom of the stationery box.
6. Close the box and leave it closed for a day or more until the paper has absorbed the scent.

·II·
Crazy Cure-Alls

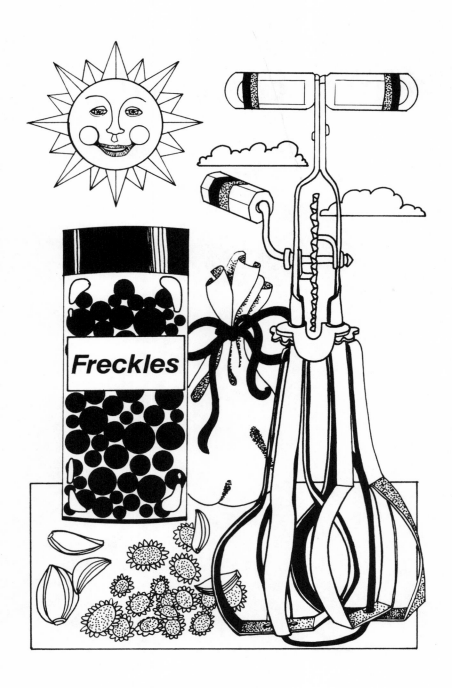

Pure and Sure Cures

For indigestion, chew parsley.
For strength, eat thyme with your meal.
For colds, drink camomile or sage tea.
For attracting money, carry basil in your pockets.
For staying young, smell rosemary frequently.
For easing sadness, sleep on a pillow stuffed with thyme.
For fresh-smelling closets, put lemon peel and rosemary in
    the corners.
For blemishes, apply bruised leaves of watercress.

To Keep Pests Away

FOR INSECTS

What You Need

Ingredients	Tools
1 cup water	cooking pot
2 teaspoons dried camomile	strainer
	jar
	sponge

What You Do

1. Boil water in cooking pot.
2. Add camomile and take pot off the stove.
3. Let mixture cool for five minutes.
4. Pour through strainer into jar.
5. Soak sponge in mixture and sponge onto body.

FOR DOG AND CAT FLEAS

What You Need

Ingredients
1 cup of dried mint leaves

Tools
handkerchief
piece of string or
  rubber band

What You Do

1. Put mint leaves in the center of the handkerchief.
2. Bring the four corners of the handkerchief toward the center and tie with the string or rubber band.
3. Place this wherever your animal sleeps.

FOR PEOPLE YOU DON'T LIKE

What You Need

Ingredients
2 or 3 cloves of garlic

Tools
pin
string

What You Do

1. Make small holes in the garlic cloves with the pin.
2. Run the string through the garlic.
3. Tie the ends of the string together.
4. Wear this around your neck.

To Remove Freckles

What You Need

Ingredients
½ cup watercress leaves
1 pint white vinegar
juice of 1 lemon
lots of freckles

Tools
large bowl
strainer
wide-mouth jar

What You Do

1. Mix all ingredients in bowl.
2. Set bowl uncovered in the sun for 3 days.
3. Pour mixture through strainer into jar.
4. Wash freckled area with mixture daily. Keep out of eyes.
5. Hope for freckles to disappear in 5 days. If not, try something else.

To Stop Baldness

What You Need

Ingredients
¼ cup sage
¼ cup rosemary
½ onion
2 tablespoons wheat germ
1 quart witch hazel

Tools
large jar
attractive covered jar
strainer

What You Do

1. Put sage, rosemary, onion and wheat germ in large jar.
2. Pour witch hazel into jar and let mixture sit uncovered for 4 days.
3. Pour mixture through strainer into gift jar.
4. Present jar to a needy father, relative or friend with the following directions:
   Apply to dry scalp and massage gently.
   Rinse off and wash scalp with clear water.
   Use daily.
   If baldness continues, see a wigmaker.

To Stop Fatness

What You Need

Ingredients

2 tablespoons fennel seed or
   sassafras
4 cups boiling water
fresh watercress leaves

Tools

teapot

What You Do

1. Rinse teapot with hot water.
2. Place fennel seeds in teapot.
3. Pour in the boiling water.
4. Cover the pot and let it steep for 10 minutes.
5. Drink a cup of this tea a day.
6. Chew fresh watercress before meals.

For Sore Feet

What You Need

Ingredients
4 cups water
½ cup dry mustard
2 tablespoons lavender

Tools
cooking pot
handkerchief
piece of string
pail

What You Do

1. Boil the water in cooking pot.
2. Place mustard and lavender in the center of the handkerchief.
3. Bring the four corners toward the center and tie with the string.
4. Drop the bag into the boiling water and boil for ten minutes.
5. Pour this water into the pail and add *cold* water.
6. Soak each foot until it feels warm.

To Cool and Refresh Skin

What You Need

Ingredients
½ cup spearmint leaves
¼ cup marjoram
¼ cup lavender

Tools
small washcloth
piece of string or rubber
band

What You Do

1. Mix the herbs and put in the center of the washcloth.
2. Pull the four corners of cloth toward the center and tie with string or rubber band.
3. Hang this bag under the spout of the bathtub.
4. Run bath water through the bag and, when tub is filled, drop the tied bag into the water.
5. Soak for 10 to 15 minutes in the tub.

To Stop Bad Breath

What You Need

Ingredients
1 cup water
2 teaspoons sage leaves
2 teaspoons mint leaves
2 teaspoons parsley

Tools
cooking pot
spoon
strainer
jar

What You Do

1. Boil the water in the cooking pot.
2. Stir all the ingredients into the water.
3. Let the mixture cool for 10 minutes.
4. Pour mixture through a strainer into the jar.
5. To use, rinse your mouth with this mixture.

For Blemished Skin

What You Need

Ingredients
1 egg
1 tablespoon honey
1 tablespoon wheat germ
¼ teaspoon mint extract

Tools
bowl
egg beater

What You Do

1. Crack the egg and put only the white in a bowl. (Save the yellow to use in Herb Shampoo or Scrambled Eggs and Herbs.)
2. Beat the egg white until it becomes stiff.
3. Add honey, wheat germ and mint extract and mix.
4. Smooth over your face and allow to dry for 15 minutes.
5. Rinse off with warm water, then rinse with cool water.
6. Repeat every week.

For Aching Muscles

What You Need

Ingredients
4 teaspoons oil of camphor
1 teaspoon oil of cloves
2 teaspoons oil of wintergreen
2 teaspoons oil of eucalyptus

Tools
jar with lid
cotton pads

What You Do

1. Pour all the ingredients into the jar.
2. Cover and shake well.
3. Dip cotton pads into mixture and spread over sore muscles.
4. Shake well before each use.

To Make Hair Shiny

What You Need

Ingredients

1 quart water
½ cup dried camomile flowers

Tools

cooking pot
strainer
container with pouring
 spout

What You Do

1. Boil water in cooking pot.
2. Put camomile flowers in water and let sit for 10 minutes.
3. Pour through the strainer into the other container with spout.
4. Pour the mixture over freshly washed hair.
5. Leave on 10 minutes and then rinse out.
6. Continue drying your hair as usual.

To Stop Dandruff

What You Do

Ingredients
1 quart of water
¼ cup camomile leaves
¼ cup rosemary

Tools
large cooking pot
handkerchief
piece of string or rubber
band

What You Do

1. Boil water in cooking pot.
2. Put herb ingredients in the center of the handkerchief.
3. Bring the four corners of the cloth toward the center and tie with string or rubber band.
4. Take pot off the fire and drop the bag into the water.
5. Allow to stand off the fire for 20 minutes in order to cool.
6. Remove the bag and rinse freshly washed hair with the herb water.

·III·
Food Recipes

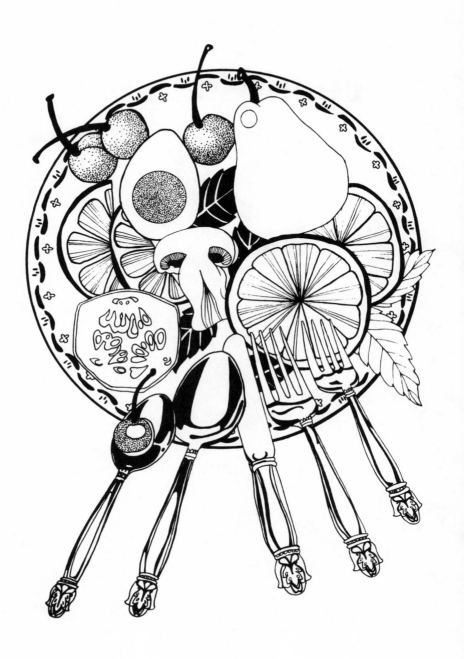

DRINKS

Herb Mint Tea

What You Need

Ingredients

1 to 2 tablespoons mint
    leaves
4 cups boiling water

Tools

teapot

What You Do

1. Rinse the teapot with hot water.
2. Place leaves in the teapot.
3. Pour in the 4 cups of boiling water.
4. Cover the pot and let steep for at least 5 minutes before pouring. Pour slowly and the leaves will remain at the bottom of the pot. Serves 4.

Herb Tomato Juice

What You Need

Ingredients
1 6-ounce can cold tomato
    juice
½ teaspoon chopped
    fresh dill

Tools
8-ounce glass
spoon

What You Do

1. Put dill in glass.
2. Pour tomato juice over dill.
3. Stir with spoon.

Summer Thirst Quencher

What You Need

Ingredients
6 ounces apricot nectar
6 ounces apple juice
¼ teaspoon cinnamon
ice cubes
mint leaves

Tools
pitcher
spoon
drinking glasses

What You Do

1. Combine apricot nectar and apple juice in pitcher.
2. Stir in cinnamon.
3. Fill glasses with ice cubes. Pour in juice. Sprinkle with
    mint leaves.

Party Ice Cubes

What You Need

Ingredients
water
herb leaves: rosehip
  and spearmint

Tools
ice-cube tray

What You Do

1. Fill ice-cube tray half full of water and let it freeze.
2. Add herb leaf to each cube and put tray back in freezer for 15 minutes.
3. Fill the tray with water. Keep tray in freezer until cubes are hard.
4. Use in drinks. Great for lemonade, punch, iced tea. Looks pretty and adds a nice taste.

SWEETS and THINGS

Herb Jelly

What You Need

Ingredients
3½ cups sugar
2 cups grape juice
⅓ cup liquid pectin
3 or 4 mint leaves or
   3 or 4 lemon-balm
   leaves

Tools
large pot
spoon
jelly jars (baby jars or
   canning jars from a
   hardware store)

What You Do

1. Mix sugar and grape juice in pot and slowly bring to a boil.
2. Stir in pectin and herb leaves.
3. Bring to a boil and boil hard for one minute.
4. Turn heat down. Stirring constantly, cook for 20 to 25 minutes.
5. Skim off foam and mint leaves with spoon.
6. Pour into jelly jars, cap and cool in refrigerator. Makes about 2 pints.

Mint Pear Jelly

What You Need

Ingredients
3 very ripe fresh pears
  (½ cup when mashed)
1 cup sugar
4 or 5 dried mint leaves
⅓ cup liquid fruit pectin

Tools
knife
bowl
spoon
large pot
jelly jars (baby jars or
  canning jars from a
  hardware store)

What You Do

1. Peel and core fresh pears.
2. In mixing bowl, mash pears until all the lumps are out.
3. Stir in sugar and mint leaves.
4. Pour mixture into pot and slowly bring to a boil.
5. Pour in pectin. Bring to a boil and cook another minute or two.
6. Skim foam and mint leaves off the top with a spoon.
7. Pour into jelly jars, cap and cool. Makes about 1 pint.

Glazed Candy Apples

What You Need

Ingredients
2 tablespoons honey
¼ teaspoon cinnamon
¼ teaspoon nutmeg
2 fresh apples

Tools
small bowl
popsicle sticks
  or forks
plate
small bowl

What You Do

1. Mix honey, cinnamon and nutmeg in bowl.
2. Push stick or fork into apples. Make sure apples are on good and tight.
3. Do one apple at a time. Dip apple into mixture. Roll the apple to coat completely.
4. Put apples with the sticks or forks facing up, on plate.
5. Put the plate in the refrigerator to harden glaze. Allow 1 hour.

Rosehip Cookies

What You Need

Ingredients
½ cup butter
½ cup sugar
1 beaten egg
½ teaspoon salt
2 teaspoons plain rose
   water*
1 pinch nutmeg
1 teaspoon rosehips
1⅓ cups flour
confectioners sugar

Tools
large mixing bowl
large spoon
blender
cookie sheet
spatula

What You Do

1. Blend butter and sugar in the bowl till fluffy.
2. Add egg, salt, rose water, and nutmeg.
3. Put rosehips in blender. Set dial on "chop" or "mix." Leave blender on for 1 minute.
4. Blend in flour and rosehips to egg mixture.
5. Grease cookie sheet.
6. Drop batter by spoonful onto cookie sheet. Batter should be stiff enough to hold its shape. If it is not, add a little more flour.
7. Bake at 375° for 10 to 15 minutes until brown on edges.
8. Remove cookies from sheet with spatula and lightly sprinkle each one with confectioners sugar. Makes 24 cookies.

*Rose water can be bought at your local pharmacy.

Sesame Popcorn Balls

What You Need

Ingredients
5 cups freshly popped corn
salt
⅓ cup sesame seeds
1 cup brown sugar
½ cup honey
½ cup hot water
3 teaspoons cinnamon
2 tablespoons butter

Tools
large bowl
spoon
pot
waxed paper

What You Do

1. Put popcorn in bowl, sprinkle with salt and sesame seeds. Mix well.
2. Melt sugar in pot and then add honey, hot water, cinnamon, and butter.
3. Cook slowly about 5 minutes. Test to see if the syrup is thick enough by dropping a little into cold water. If it makes a soft ball, it is ready.
4. Pour syrup over popcorn and mix gently with a spoon.
5. Butter your hands and shape popcorn into balls. Place on waxed paper.
6. Allow the popcorn balls to cool and harden. Makes 6 medium-sized balls.

Mint Orange Delight

What You Need

Ingredients
4 oranges
2 tablespoons honey
¼ cup water
shredded coconut
fresh or dried mint
cinnamon
4 cherries (fresh or bottled)

Tools
4 dessert dishes
small pot

What You Do

1. Peel oranges and separate into sections.
2. Place even amounts of orange sections in dishes.
3. Mix honey and water in pot. Warm and stir for three or four minutes.
4. Pour honey-water mixture over each dish of oranges.
5. Sprinkle coconut and mint leaves over each dish.
6. To each dish add a dash of cinnamon and top with a cherry. Serves 4.

Alphabet Pretzels

What You Need

Ingredients
4 packages dry yeast
1¼ cups warm water
4 cups flour
1 tablespoon sugar
1 teaspoon salt
1 egg slightly beaten
¼ cup coarse-grained salt
poppy seeds or dill seeds or
    caraway seeds

Tools
large bowls (2)
greased cookie sheet

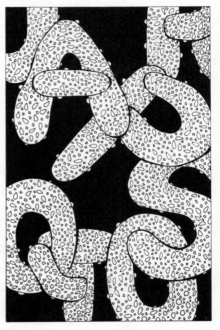

What You Do

1. Dissolve the yeast in the warm water in one bowl.
2. Combine flour, sugar and salt in other bowl.
3. Work 3 cups of the flour mixture into the yeast mixture.
4. Begin to knead and then add remaining flour mixture.
5. Separate the dough into small pieces. Use your hands to roll into thin snakelike shapes.
6. Shape into letters and place on cookie sheet. Make your initials or a friend's initials.
7. Brush letters with beaten egg.

8. Sprinkle letters with coarse-grained salt and whichever seeds you want to use.
9. Bake at 425° for 20 minutes or until brown. Makes 12 large or 24 small pretzels.
10. To give as a gift, place in small plastic bag. Tie with a ribbon.

Mint Candy

What You Need

Ingredients
2 egg whites
6 drops oil of wintergreen
3 ½ cups confectioners sugar

Tools
bowl
fork or whisk
waxed paper
rolling pin
knife or cookie cutter

What You Do

1. Beat the egg whites lightly with a fork or whisk. (Save the yellow to use in Summer Thirst Quencher or Lemon Pancakes.)
2. Slowly drop the oil of wintergreen into egg whites.
3. Gradually beat in the sugar, little by little.
4. Be sure mixture is well blended and roll it out on waxed paper.
5. Cut the candy into small rounds. (You can use a knife, a cookie cutter or a small bottle cap to shape the candy.)
6. Allow the candy to harden and become dry. Makes about 12 small candies.

MEALTIME HELPERS

Lemon Pancakes

What You Need

Ingredients
1 egg
¼ cup milk
¼ cup plain yogurt
2 tablespoons oil
1 cup flour
2 teaspoons baking
   powder
1 tablespoon sugar
1 tablespoon bottled
   grated lemon peel
½ teaspoon crushed
   coriander
a pat of butter, and honey
   to pour on pancakes

Tools
bowl
spoon
greased frying pan
spatula

What You Do

1. Mix egg, milk, yogurt, and oil in bowl and beat lightly.
2. Add the flour, baking powder, sugar, lemon peel and coriander. Stir this mixture and add more milk if you like thinner pancakes.
3. Spoon the batter onto hot frying pan. When the cakes are full of bubbles, turn over with spatula. Cook until brown on the other side. Top with butter and pour honey over pancakes. Serve hot. Makes about 12 medium-sized pancakes.

Scrambled Eggs and Herbs

What You Need

Ingredients
1 or 2 eggs
1 teaspoon milk
¼ teaspoon salt
a pinch basil, parsley,
    oregano, paprika or
    your choice of herb
1 tablespoon butter

Tools
bowl
spoon
frying pan

What You Do

1. Crack eggs in bowl.
2. Add milk to eggs.
3. Add salt and as many herbs as you like.
4. Beat all together.
5. Melt butter in the frying pan and cook the eggs,
   stirring until they are solid but soft.

Cinnamon French Toast

What You Need

Ingredients
1 egg
¼ cup milk
¼ teaspoon cinnamon
⅛ teaspoon salt
1 tablespoon butter
2 slices white bread

Tools
bowl
fork
frying pan
spatula

What You Do

1. Crack egg into bowl.
2. Put milk, cinnamon, salt in bowl. Beat well with fork.
3. Heat butter in frying pan.
4. Dip each slice of bread in mixture. First one side, then the other.
5. Put the 2 slices of bread in the pan.
6. Cook 4 minutes on each side, turning with spatula.

Herb French Bread

What You Need

Ingredients

6 tablespoons soft butter or
   margarine
1 tablespoon parsley
$\frac{1}{2}$ teaspoon oregano
$\frac{1}{2}$ teaspoon basil
1 loaf of unsliced French
   bread

Tools

bowl
cutting knife
cookie sheet

What You Do

1. Set oven to 400 degrees.
2. Mix butter with herbs in a bowl.
3. Cut loaf of French bread in half lengthwise, making 2 long pieces.
4. Place both pieces of bread on cookie sheet, crust side down.
5. Spread butter-herb mixture over top of each piece of bread.
6. Place cookie sheet in middle of oven.
7. Bake for 15 minutes or until bread is crusty.
8. Remove from oven. Cut into slices and serve hot.

Herbal Dip for Raw Vegetables

What You Need

Ingredients
½ cup yogurt
½ cup sour cream
2 tablespoons honey
1 teaspoon parsley
1 teaspoon dill seed
raw vegetables of your
    choice: celery, carrots,
    cucumbers, green
    peppers, tomatoes

Tools
bowl
spoon
knife

What You Do

1. In the bowl, mix all ingredients
   except the vegetables. Refrigerate for 1 hour or more.
2. Wash and slice the vegetables.
3. Dip them in dressing and eat.

Herb Salt

What You Need

Ingredients
¼ cup chopped parsley
1 teaspoon dried basil
1 teaspoon dried oregano
1 teaspoon paprika
1 cup salt

Tools
small bowl
salt shaker

What You Do

1. Crumble the herbs until they are fine.
2. Combine all ingredients in bowl.
3. Pour into shaker. Makes your hamburgers taste real yummy.

Herb Butters
Parsley, Dill, or Oregano Butter

What You Need

Ingredients
¼ pound salt butter
2 tablespoons chopped
   herbs—choose one

Tools
small bowl
fork

What You Do

1. Take butter out of refrigerator and allow to soften for 20 minutes.
2. Place butter and herbs in bowl.
3. Mix well with fork and chill.

·IV·
Growing Herbs

Tips

Before You Plant Your Herbs Check These Tips Out

1. Make sure you choose a sunny spot. Herbs love sun.
2. Herbs can grow anywhere. They can be a border in your family garden or they can be a garden all by themselves. You can plant them in a patch the size of a hopscotch court—or you can plant them in a field. If you are making a special herb garden, the best is a 3' x 5' area.
3. If you can find a place near your kitchen door—great!
4. Fencing—whatever you choose.
5. Water—herbs must have a drink once or twice a week.
6. If this is your first try at gardening, select herbs that will grow easily.

Growing Your Own Outdoor Herb Garden

PLANTING HERBS THAT COME IN PEAT POTS

What You Need

Ingredients
a sunny garden spot
water
herb plants in peat pots

Tools
metal rake
long stick or tree branch
trowel
water hose with spray attachment, or if this is not available, use a watering can

What You Do

1. Turn over grass to expose soil. Rake soil until all the lumps and stones are loose.
2. Rake again until soil is clear of stones and lumps.
3. With stick or branch make rows.
4. Dig a hole with the trowel bigger than the pot the plant is in.
5. Put dirt to one side of hole.
6. Fill hole with water; then place entire peat pot in hole.
7. Replace dirt around plant and pot.
8. Press soil down firmly.
9. Take the name stick that is in pot and put it right next to plant in the ground.
10. Once a week water plant with spray from hose or watering can.

PLANTING HERBS THAT COME IN CLAY POTS

What You Do

Follow the same instructions as given for planting herbs in peat pots. This time, however, herb plants must be taken out of pot before planting. When you do this you must be very careful not to harm the roots. You should try to remove the plant and all the dirt in one piece.

The way to do this is to gently knock pot against the ground once or twice. Next place one hand over the plant. The herb plant should just slide out.

GROWING HERBS FROM SEEDS

What You Need

Ingredients
a sunny garden spot
water
herb seeds

Tools
metal rake
long stick or tree branch
stapling machine
small twigs
water hose with spray attachment,
    or if this is not available,
    use a watering can

What You Do

1. Turn over grass to expose soil. Rake soil until all the lumps and stones are loose.
2. With long stick make rows.
3. Follow instructions on packet, because each herb has its own seed depth. The packet will also tell you how close together to place the seeds.
4. Put seeds in ground. Press the soil over them firmly.
5. Staple empty seed packet to twig, so that you will be able to easily identify the herbs that you've planted.
6. Water well with spray from hose or watering can.

Indoor Herb Clay Pots

What You Need

Ingredients
sand
soil
herb plant or seed

Tools
clay pots
large spoon
spray mister

What You Do

1. Mix sand and soil, using one measure of sand for every two measures of soil.
2. Fill clay pots three-quarters full.
3. Place the plant or seed in each pot.
4. For a seed, cover with soil mixture.
5. Water once a week.
6. In addition, mist three times a week to keep from drying out.

Drying Herbs

Method 1

After a roast has been cooked in the oven, the oven is just right for drying your herbs.

1. Spread herbs on a clean cookie sheet.
2. Place cookie sheet in the warm oven. (Be sure oven is turned off.)
3. Leave for 10 to 15 minutes until the leaves are crisp.
4. Place dried herbs in clear glass containers. Clean baby-food jars are perfect for this.

Method 2

1. Cut herb plant at the base of the stem.
2. Tie in bunches.
3. Hang in bunches upside down in a cool dry place until they are dry and crumbly.
4. Put in clean containers.

Easy and Tasty Kinds of Herbs

There are two kinds of herbs. Perennials come up every year after you plant them. Annuals last for one season.

Perennial

Mint: There are many varieties of mint. The most popular are spearmint and peppermint. Mint is very easy to grow. Buy plants. The more you cut them the more they will grow. You can use mint either fresh or dried.

Oregano: Buy the "Italian" kind. You can use it either fresh or dried. It will make your spaghetti sauce or pizza taste extra special.

Thyme: Buy the plant. It is a sweet-smelling plant. When you cook eggs or fish, snip some thyme and use it as seasoning.

Chives: You can buy pots of chives from a nursery. They come in a bunch of little bulbs. Separate them. Each bulb sends up tasty leaves which you snip.

Lavender: (*Lavandula vera*) grows to about 1 inch. It is gray-green in color with lovely small lavender flowers.

Annual

Parsley: Comes in many varieties—buy any variety that suits you. It has many, many uses. There is at least three times more vitamin C in parsley than in orange juice.

Basil: Choose any variety. Usually you will have to buy

the seed packets. Follow directions on package. It is hardy and you should have little difficulty growing it.

Dill: A tall plant with feathery leaves and yellow flowers. Dill needs to be watered twice a week. Fresh dill makes potato salad extra special.

Where To Buy Herb Seeds and Plants

First try your local seed stores and nurseries. If you can't find what you want there, write away for a catalog from one of the places listed below. This is by no means a complete list; it is just to get you started.

W. Atlee Burpee Company
Warminster, Pennsylvania 18991

Casa Yerba
Star Route 2, Box 21
Day's Creek, Oregon 97429

Hemlock Hill Herb Farms
Litchfield, Connecticut 06759

Hill Top Herb Farm
Box 866
Cleveland, Texas 77327
Catalog 30¢

Merry Gardens
Camden, Maine 04843
Catalog 25¢

Nichols Garden Nursery
1190 North Pacific Highway
Albany, Oregon 97321

Penn Herb Co.
603 North Second Street
Philadelphia, Pennsylvania 19147

Sunnybrook Farms Nursery
9448 Mayfield Road
Chesterland, Ohio 44026

The Tool Shed Herb Farm
Turkey Hill Road
Salem Center
Purdys Station, N.Y. 10578
Catalog 25¢

Dried herbs and herb oils can also be bought in health food stores and groceries. If you cannot find them locally, you may order them from these places:

Caswell-Massey Company, Inc.
320 West 13th Street
New York, N.Y. 10010

Nature's Herb Company
281 Ellis Street
San Francisco, California 94102

Index